W9-BXU-437

good answers
to tough questions

About Death

FRANKLIN PIERCE
COLLEGE LIBRARY
RINDGE, N.H. 03461

Dedicated to my father,
Richard Jackson Berry,
who died while this book was being written.

Written by Joy Berry

CHILDRENS PRESS ®

CHICAGO

CURR
HQ
1073.3
.B47
1990

Managing Editor: Lana Eberhard

Copy Editor: Annette Gooch

Contributing Editors: Margie Austin, John Bilitch, Ph.D.,
Libby Byers, Ilene Frommer, James Gough, M.D., Dan Gurney,
Charles Pengra, Ph.D., Howard Perlman, Michael Thomas

Contributing Writer: Annette Gooch

Designer: Jennifer Wiezel

Illustration Designer: Bartholomew

Inking Artist: Micah Schwaberow

Lettering Artist: Linda Hanney

Coloring Artist: Berenice Happé Iriks

Typography and Production: Communication Graphics

Published by Childrens Press
in cooperation with Living Skills Press

This book can answer the following questions about death:
- What is death?
- What causes death?
- What is it like to die?
- Why do people die?
- How do people feel about death?
- How do people react when they discover they are about to die?
- What rights are dying people entitled to?
- What happens to the human body after death?
- What happens to the human spirit after death?
- How can you prepare yourself to die?

Like all living things, every human being has a lifetime.

A lifetime includes a
- birth,
- life, and
- death.

At birth, a human being begins its life.

At the end of his or her life, a human being experiences death.

When death occurs, these things happen:
- the heart stops functioning, and blood is no longer circulated to the brain;
- without nourishment from the blood to fuel it, the brain stops functioning; and
- without messages from the brain to tell it what do do, the body stops functioning.

The process that leads to death is called **dying**. To experience death is to **die**. When death occurs, the body **dies**. A dead body is called a **corpse**.

EVERYONE, INCLUDING MY GRANDFATHER, KNEW THAT HE WAS GOING TO DIE SOON.

Several things can cause death. The *aging process* can cause death. As a person grows older, the body gradually wears out until it can no longer function.

MY GRANDFATHER DIED BECAUSE HE WAS VERY OLD.

A *major illness* can cause death. The four major illnesses that cause the greatest number of deaths are

- cancer,
- heart attacks,
- strokes, and
- pneumonia.

Influenza also causes many deaths in old people.

An *accident* can cause death. Fatal accidents are often related to
- transportation (automobiles, airplanes, trains),
- work, or
- recreation.

A *disaster* can cause death. Disasters are either
- natural disasters (earthquakes, tornadoes, tidal waves, floods) or
- man-made disasters (wars, fires, explosions).

I'VE HEARD ABOUT PEOPLE DYING BECAUSE OF A DISASTER.

Physical assaults can cause death. Fatal physical assaults are usually
- suicides or
- murders.

Euthanasia is a cause of death. Euthanasia is also called *mercy killing*. Mercy killing is the act of taking the life of someone who is thought to be incurably ill or injured so that the person will suffer as little as possible.

Passive euthanasia is discontinuing medical treatment and/or turning off medical equipment used to keep a person alive.

Active euthanasia is giving a lethal dose of a drug to a person or using some other means to end his or her life.

AT THE PRESENT TIME, MERCY KILLING IS NOT LEGAL. SOME PEOPLE THINK THAT IT SHOULD BE. WHAT DO YOU THINK?

It is impossible to know exactly what it is like to die because it is not possible to converse with anyone who has died. However, death is apparently something every person can handle because it is natural and eventually happens to every human being.

It also seems likely that death is painless because only a body that is alive and functioning can experience pain.

There is only so much space on the earth. Therefore, only a limited number of people can live on it comfortably. When people die, they make room for the people who are being born.

There are only so many resources, such as food and water, available to meet the needs of people who live on the earth. When people die, the resources they would have used become available to the people who are still living.

THERE WOULD NOT BE ENOUGH RESOURCES IN THE WORLD TO KEEP EVERYONE ALIVE IF NO ONE DIED.

The earth and everything on it are made up of elements. When someone dies, the elements that make up a person's body become part of the earth and air and are used to create new things. Thus, death is a necessary part of a recycling of the earth's elements.

Death often spares very old people from having to continue living after they have grown tired and weary of coping with the problems, pain, and losses that are a part of living.

Anything in unlimited supply is often taken for granted and seldom appreciated or enjoyed as much as it could be. The realization that people have only a limited amount of time to live often causes them to *appreciate* and *enjoy* the time they have.

Also, the realization that people have only a limited amount of time to live often causes them to **value** the time they have. People who value their time use it wisely and usually productively. Productive people are happier and more contented than those who are not.

Some very old or very sick people want to die. However, most people do not look forward to dying.

Many people fear dying because they do not know what death will be like.

Because people do not know what it is like to die, they often make up their own thoughts about it. These thoughts can cause people to experience extremely uncomfortable feelings.

Some people fear dying because they think death will be
- painful,
- frightening, or
- lonely.

People who are about to die usually go through five stages in dealing with it.

Stage One — Denial
During this stage, people who are close to death refuse to believe or accept that they are dying.

Stage Two — Anger

During this stage, people often feel angry because they think it is unfair that they have to die while other people can continue to live.

Stage Three — Bargaining
During this stage, people often try to negotiate with whatever force they think has control over life and death. For example, people who believe in God might promise to live better lives if they are allowed to continue living.

Stage Four — Depression

During this stage, people often regret the bad things they did and the good things they failed to do during their lifetime. They also feel sad about the people they can no longer be with and the things they can no longer do once they are dead.

Stage Five — Acceptance
During this stage, people accept that they are dying and prepare themselves to die.

Throughout all five stages, most people who are close to death remain *hopeful* that something might happen to change things. For example, people with incurable diseases usually hope that a cure will be discovered in time to save their lives.

MY AUNT ALWAYS HOPED THAT SOMEONE WOULD COME UP WITH SOMETHING TO MAKE HER WELL AGAIN.

Dying people have the right to
- be treated as living human beings until they die,
- honestly express their thoughts and feelings about their life and death,
- maintain a sense of hopefulness,
- discuss and possibly change their religious or spiritual beliefs in any way that will make death more tolerable for them,
- have their questions answered honestly and not be deceived by others, and
- surround themselves with people who will support them and help them face death.

Dying people also have the right to
- participate in decisions concerning their care;
- be cared for by individuals who are not only knowledgeable and competent but sensitive and caring as well;
- expect continuing medical and nursing attention, even when getting well is no longer possible;
- do whatever is necessary to be free from pain and mental anguish;
- die where they choose, surrounded by people they choose to have with them at their time of death; and
- decide what is to be done with their bodies after death and be assured that their decisions will be respected and implemented.

Some people decide to become *organ donors*.

After death, an organ donor's body is taken to a place where doctors remove one or more body parts. These are then put into the bodies of people who have malfunctioning body parts that need to be replaced.

I CARRY THIS CARD IN MY WALLET. IT LETS PEOPLE KNOW THAT IF I DIE, I WANT MY ORGANS TO BE USED BY SOMEONE WHO NEEDS THEM.

Some people decide they want their bodies to be *embalmed*.

After death, the blood is drained from the body and replaced with embalming fluid. The embalming fluid preserves the body by slowing down the process of decay. The embalmed body is then either interred, entombed, or used for medical research.

After death, the body is placed in a **casket** (a box large enough to hold a human body). The casket is then buried in a **grave** (a hole dug in the ground). Some graves contain a **grave receptacle** (a concrete vault or liner that protects the casket). Most graves are in burial grounds called **cemeteries** or **graveyards**. A **gravestone** or **tombstone** is a marker placed on top of a grave site to indicate whose body is buried there.

Some people choose **entombment**.

After death, the body is placed in a casket. The casket is then put into a **crypt** (a special chamber or vault). The crypt is within a **mausoleum** (an above-ground structure or building that holds caskets). There are **individual mausoleums** that hold single caskets and **family mausoleums** that hold many caskets. Mausoleums are usually in cemeteries. A **face plate** is a marker placed on a crypt to indicate whose body is buried there.

Some people decide to be **buried at sea**.

After death, the body is placed in a weighted casket or **body bag** (a bag large enough to hold a human body). The casket or body bag is taken out to sea by boat. Then it is placed in the water, where it sinks to the bottom of the ocean.

Some people decide they want their bodies used for *medical research*.

After death, the body is taken to a medical school where students use it to study the human body.

Some people decide to be *cremated*.

After death, the body is taken to a *crematorium* (a place where it undergoes *cremation*). During cremation, the body is reduced to *ashes* by being burned at very high heat. This process takes approximately six to eight hours.

Ashes from a cremation can be
- placed in a grave or crypt,
- scattered in designated places or into the ocean, or
- placed in a container called an **urn** and kept by a friend or relative.

The human *spirit* is everything about a person except his or her body. It is a person's feelings, thoughts, and personality. Sometimes the spirit is called the *soul*.

Some people believe that when the body dies, the spirit no longer exists.

Some people believe that when the body dies, the spirit leaves the body and goes to a place of reward or a place of punishment. They also believe that where people's spirits go depends upon decisions the people made or things they did while they were alive.

SOME PEOPLE BELIEVE THE SPIRIT GOES TO A PLACE CALLED HEAVEN OR A PLACE CALLED HELL.

HMMM...

Some people believe that when the body dies, the spirit *reincarnates*. This means that the spirit becomes a part of other living things such as humans, animals, or plants.

SOME PEOPLE BELIEVE THE SPIRIT BECOMES PART OF OTHER LIVING THINGS.

People who prepare themselves to die seem to handle dying better than people who do not. No matter how young or old a person is, there are things he or she can do to prepare for death.

To prepare yourself for death, you might want to **make sure all your questions about death are answered**.
- Think of all the questions you have about death.
- Make a list of your questions.
- Do your best to have your questions answered. You might need to talk to people or read books and articles about death.

IT'S **iMPORTANT** FOR YOU TO KNOW ALL YOU CAN ABOUT DEATH.

To prepare yourself for death, you might also want to **write a will**. A **will** is a document that explains what you want done with your possessions after you die.

- A will can include instructions for what should be done with your body and what kind of funeral or memorial service should be arranged after you die.
- You should review your will every year to make sure it is accurate and up to date.
- You should also let other people know where your will is kept.

These facts are known to be true:
- Death is **necessary** to the survival of the human population.
- Death is a **natural** part of human existence.
- Death is an **inevitable** part of every human being's lifetime.

The answers to these questions cannot be known:
- What is the exact time a person is going to die?
- Why do some people die young while other people die old?
- Why do "good" people sometimes die tragic deaths while "bad" people are allowed to continue to live?

IT'S NOT THE LENGTH OF A PERSON'S LIFE THAT MATTERS. IT IS THE QUALITY OF A PERSON'S LIFE THAT MATTERS. IN OTHER WORDS, SOME PEOPLE LIVE WONDERFUL SHORT LIVES WHILE OTHERS LIVE LONG, MISERABLE LIVES.

Learning what you can about death might motivate you to live a happier, more productive life. Having some unanswered questions about death can preserve the "mystery of life" and make your lifetime an exciting adventure.

I HOPE THIS DISCUSSION ABOUT DEATH WILL HELP YOU WANT TO DO WHATEVER IS NECESSARY TO MAKE YOUR LIFE AS WONDERFUL AS IT CAN BE.